Published by Palphot Ltd.
P.O.Box 2, Herzlia 46100, Israel
Tel. 09-9525252, Fax: 09-9525277
ISBN 965-280-057-8

Printed by Israphot, Karney Shomron

Culinary Editor: Nurit Branitzky
Photography: Nelly Sheffer
Props and Food Styling: Nurit Branitzky
Design: Noga Moscovic

Other Photographs: N. Sheffer, Garo Nalbandian,
L. Borodulin, Abrams Photo-Graphics,
S. Mendrea, E. Lessing, N. Lev.

The Melting Pot

A Quick and Easy Blend of Israeli Cuisine

by
Tami Lehman-Wilzig
&
Miriam Blum

PUBLISHED BY PALPHOT LTD.

"So What's Cooking?"

What's new on the Israeli menu? There must be a satiating answer to this question.

As opposed to French, Italian or Chinese cuisine, Israeli cooking cannot be strictly defined by specific condiments, flavors, or dishes. While Israel's geographic location has provided the country's victuals with a decided Middle Eastern orientation, socially Israel is a state whose population represents 80 countries from both East and West, meeting in the same melting pot. And while it's a nation not yet 50 years old, it boasts a two thousand year old culinary credo which began when the Jews were dispersed to the four corners of the earth. Once the nation was finally reunited, several international ingredients came together under one lid serving up the most memorable meals, many of which are based on recipe variations. Who can kvetch about a cauldron dishing out "Gvetch" - a favorite Eastern European vegetable dish; "Mejadra" - a Galilean Arab lentil and rice combination which has its own Yemenite variation; famous one-course meals such as the Iraqi "Kubeh," Moroccan "Couscous," and the European "Cholent"; Syrian-style string beans; creamy French quiches; and all-American apple pie - served with Turkish coffee, of course!

Whereas outdoor wining and dining was once synonymous with catching a quick falafel and a

can of soda, hailing falafel as Israel's national dish is a thing of the past. Certainly, the population still enjoys a variety of street foods gulped on the run. Still, today's urbane Israeli revels in the experience of feasting in restaurants. Eateries of all types. Hungarian. Oriental. French. Chinese. You'll find a matching restaurant for every major country where Jews have planted roots.

Which is not to say that true Israeli cuisine is found only in restaurants. Authentic Israeli cooking boils, simmers and bakes at home. While Israelis hailing from all over the world preserve their original cooking traditions, daily friendly exchanges with next door neighbors makes it easy to incorporate and adapt recipes of other civilizations into their daily menu. The end result? Israelis of European descent are cooking fish with tehina, slicing, frying and seasoning eggplants into savory salad servings, while their Middle Eastern counterparts are making schnitzel, meat goulash and cauliflower kugel.

Israelis also revere the Bible and its edicts. Aside from adhering to the Kashrut laws, they have applied a verbatim definition to the command "Be Fruitful and Multiply." No way connected to a citrus market, the decree prompted kibbutz farmers to tenaciously till a stubbornly arid land until it literally bore the fruits of their labor - yielding an endless supply of fresh fruits and vegetables plus a cornucopia of exotic strains - all of which are exported the world over.

Enter the famous Israeli breakfast: founded on the kibbutz, practiced in every home, honed to perfection in the country's hotels, beloved by tourists who shrewdly pack a picnic lunch at the end of the meal. What meets the eye is nothing less than a mouth-watering feast of finely cut fresh vegetables, salads, refreshing juices, freshly baked breads and rolls, dairy delights, herring and smoked fish, plus coffee and tea.

With this lavish spread starting the day, it's obvious that in Israel the traditional exhortation of every Jewish mother is alive and well, crossing all cultural lines. Considering the trim figures strolling along Tel Aviv's popular Dizengoff Street, it's hard to believe that instead of belonging to "Weight Watchers," Israelis "Wait & Watch" the clock. Seven o'clock in the morning, and it's time for breakfast. Three hours later the entire country pauses for a 10 AM snack consisting of a roll, fruit and beverage. By 1:00 PM the moment has arrived for the day's main meal - lunch - consisting of an appetizer, soup, main course (including hot grain and vegetable), plus dessert. Come 5:00 PM and the average Israeli must have a cup of coffee or tea - accompanied of course by either a luscious slice of creamy cake, a sweet fruit tart, or a salty, doughy, sesame covered piece of pastry. Thankfully, dinner is a light affair consisting of bread, assorted cheeses and yogurts, finely cut Israeli salad, plus a hot or cold drink. Fortunately or unfortunately, supper does not signal the conclusion of eating for the day. Instead of inviting guests out to a restaurant, Israelis still entertain at home.

With so much eating - and feasting - we've decided it's time to give you some food for thought. Tasty tidbits on Israeli food and eating habits, plus 42 recipes gleaned from dozens of Israeli home chefs. All compiled in this portable volume which provides you with an uncomplicated approach to Israeli cooking.

Every recipe adheres to the kashrut laws and the bill-of-fare is excitingly exotic and surprisingly easy to whip up. What's more, we've made sure the ingredients are easily accessible around the globe. Our aim is to show you that with the least bit of effort you can prepare an exotic cuisine and serve up many savory meals of palate - pleasing delights which will be devoured to the last morsel.

Once you've finished feasting over these recipes you'll have a lot to answer the next time someone asks you: "So, what's cooking?"

Salads

In terms of novelty, no one beats Israel at the salad bar. Israel is renowned for its horn of plenty thanks to its ongoing agricultural innovations and forced growing techniques which yield a cornucopia of fresh produce all year round. In turn, Israeli chefs are continuously concocting new salads and dips, some of which must be cooked and chilled before serving.

From the standpoint of versatility, salads are the ultimate dish. Israelis eat them either as a first course, light meal, or festive fare for evening entertaining. Always served with an assortment of olives, pickles and chili-based relishes, salads are a mouth-watering sight.

As a first course, small portions are served to spice up one's appetite for the oncoming repast. Interested in a light, zesty meal? Tastefully arrange a variety of salads and dips on individual dishes around the table, alongside pita bread and crackers. Evening soirees? With bowls and platters strategically placed around the room, Israelis dip into these spicy foods while conducting animated conversations.

Humus With Tehina

An integral part of Middle Eastern cuisine, humus and tehina are considered national dishes in Israel. Two favorite dips which are often combined, Israelis use pita bread to literally mop up the plate when they are served. Humus and tehina are ideal as side portions, entrees, in-between meal snacks, and garnishes for pita-filled foods such as falafel and shwarma.

INGREDIENTS

(4-6 servings)
1 cup washed chickpeas, and
1 tsp baking soda
5 tbsp lemon juice
2 crushed garlic cloves
3 tbsp olive oil
3 tbsp tehina
³/₄ tsp salt (or to taste)
¹/₂ tsp pepper
Garnish: olive oil,
prepared tehina, chopped
parsley, red paprika and
¹/₂ cup cooked chickpeas.

PREPARATION

Soak chickpeas overnight in 4 cups of hot water and baking soda.

Drain chickpeas. Put in a pan, cover with 5 cups salted water and cook for about one hour, until tender. Put ¹/₂ cup aside for garnish.

Put drained chickpeas and remaining ingredients in food processor or blender, and blend until smooth.

Taste. Add more lemon juice or salt if required.

To serve: Spread 3-4 tbsp humus on each serving plate. Place 2 tsp tehina in center and drizzle olive oil around. Garnish with parsley, paprika and chickpeas. Serve with warm pita bread.

Falafel

Back in the 1960's Israeli children sang the song "And We Have Falafel." In comparing native dishes from all over the world, the song sang the praises of this home-grown specialty. An integral part of Israeli folklore, falafel reigns supreme among the country's fast food offerings. Today's falafel stands have evolved into a "do it yourself" experience for Israelis interested in a light lunch or snack. The hot falafel balls stand amid a wide array of salad offerings from which customers can pick and choose. Nothing is more enticing than a quick falafel and pita "sandwich" packed with finely chopped cucumbers, tomatoes, cabbage, eggplant strips and chips - all topped with tehina.

INGREDIENTS

(For 60-70 balls)
2½ cups washed chickpeas
2 tsp baking soda
1 tsp crushed coriander seeds
1 tbsp chopped coriander leaves (optional)
3 crushed garlic cloves
¼ cup finely chopped parsley
1 tsp ground cumin
½ tsp cayenne pepper
2 tsp salt
¼ tsp black pepper
¼ cup flour
oil for frying

PREPARATION

Soak chickpeas overnight in 10 cups hot water and baking soda.
Drain the chickpeas.
Grind in a blender or food processor until fine. Add spices and flour. If mixture is too dry, add a few drops of water.
Make small balls about 1¼" (3 cm) in diameter. Place on waxed paper or a greased baking sheet.
Heat the oil and deep fry a few balls at a time, for 2-3 minutes until golden brown. Drain on a paper towel. Keep balls warm.
To serve: Stuff 6 balls in a fresh pita bread together with humus, tehina, fresh vegetable salad and hot pepper sauce. Eat warm.

Fried Eggplant Slices

From the beginning of Israeli statehood, eggplant has played a pivotal role in the Israeli diet. Israelis have become so adept at creating eggplant concoctions, that it is often unrecognizable. For instance, when cooked and baked together with pasta and yellow cheese, you have a savory lasagna. Grilled and mashed, it often serves as the base for a vegetarian chopped liver. This particular eggplant variation can be found at festive functions and at falafel stands.

INGREDIENTS

(4 servings)
3 medium eggplants
4 canned pimentos or
2 fresh ones, finely chopped (use gloves)
1 cup tomato ketchup
$^1/_3$ cup vinegar
3-4 crushed garlic cloves
salt & pepper to taste
oil for frying

PREPARATION

Wash and dry eggplants. Remove stems and cut crosswise into $^3/_4$" (or 2 cm) slices.

Sprinkle both sides with salt and let drain for about 30 minutes on each side. Dry with a paper towel.

Heat oil in a large, heavy skillet and fry eggplant slices until golden. Drain on paper towels.

Cut pimentos into slices and add to eggplant in a bowl.

Mix ketchup, vinegar, garlic & seasonings. Pour over eggplant.

Gently mix and chill for a few hours before serving. Can garnish with parsley.

Can be kept refrigerated for several weeks.

Avocado Dip

Along with falafel, humus, tehina and eggplant, avocado is synonymous with Israeli cuisine. Israeli avocado cultivation dates back to the early 1920's. Today, Israel claims 18,000 acres of avocado groves. To the dismay of Europeans who view avocado as a choice delicacy, many Israelis take avocado pulp and spread it on bread, much as they would butter or margarine. Nonetheless, there are many Israelis who use avocado as the base for a tasty hors d'oeuvre or dip.

INGREDIENTS

(4 servings)
2 large ripe avocados
3 hard-boiled eggs
$^1/_2$ tsp salt
$^1/_4$ tsp freshly ground black pepper
2-3 tbsp lemon juice
2 tbsp mayonnaise
1-2 finely chopped green onions or
$^1/_2$ bunch chives
Garnish: chives

PREPARATION

Halve avocados. Scoop out flesh and mash or dice. Pour lemon juice over avocados to prevent discoloring.

Mash eggs and add to avocados.

Add the remaining ingredients. For a creamier consistency, blend in a food processor.

Adjust seasonings and refrigerate.

Serve as a dip with cut vegetables and crackers, or as a first course garnished with chives.

Israeli Salad

If you're looking for a simple but typical Israeli recipe, this is it. A salad born on the kibbutz by farmers who lovingly planted and nurtured a wide variety of fresh vegetables, this dish is central to any Israeli buffet, whether it be at home, in a hotel or a restaurant. There is an art to making Israeli salad, for it requires nimble fingers capable of finely chopping and cubing the vegetables. It is a home staple for every breakfast and supper, made just before the meal.

INGREDIENTS

(4 servings)
2-4 cucumbers
4 large tomatoes
1 green pepper. Remove seeds.
1 red pepper. Remove seeds.
1 small onion
2 tbsp olive oil
1 tsp salt
1 tsp pepper
1 tbsp lemon juice

PREPARATION

Finely dice all vegetables, the smaller the better, and mix together in a bowl.

Add oil and lemon juice. Season to taste and serve immediately.

To make a richer salad than the one described above, add chopped olives, coarsely grated carrots, cubed avocado, radishes, green onions, hot peppers, thinly sliced cabbage or lettuce, grated lemon peel and chopped parsley.

Moroccan Carrot Salad

"Saba Eliezer Ve Hagezer"-"Grandpa Eliezer and the Carrot." That's the name of a favorite Israeli children's story written by Levin Kipnus. Was Grandpa growing carrots for this salad? Israelis hailing from North Africa have proven that cooked carrots need not be served hot. For spicing up a main course served on the Sabbath or holidays, this "cool" recipe is a must.

INGREDIENTS

(4 servings)
8 young carrots
2 crushed garlic cloves
$1/2$ tsp brown sugar
$1/4$ tsp curry powder
$1/4$ tsp cumin
5 tbsp lemon juice
4 tbsp chopped parsley
$3/4$ tsp salt
$1/4$ tsp pepper

PREPARATION

Peel and slice carrots.

Put in a pot and cook covered for about 10 minutes in boiling water, until tender but still crisp.

Mix remaining ingredients together with 3 tbsp of the water from the cooked carrots.

Pour the mixture over the carrots while they are still hot and toss. Adjust seasoning.

Refrigerate for a few hours before serving.

Stuffed Vine Leaves

It's Greek to us? Not at all. When it comes to making stuffed vine leaves Israelis fully understand the fine nuances of this recipe. After all, Noah started it all by planting vineyards. Rashi - the Biblical commentator - notes that "when he entered the ark he brought in with him grapevines." Today, Israelis grow grapes both in vineyards and on the grounds of private homes. Consequently, vine leaves are easily available. The fact that there are native Greek, Turkish and Lebanese Israelis also helps. After all, this is a dish indigenous to Eastern Mediterranean countries.

INGREDIENTS

(8 servings)
About 30 pickled vine leaves
1 chopped onion
4 tbsp olive oil
$^1/_2$ cup rice, washed, drained & dried
1 lb (450g) chopped meat
$^1/_4$ cup pine nuts
1 tbsp tomato sauce
salt & black pepper to taste
2 tbsp lemon juice
1 tbsp vegetable oil

PREPARATION

Soak vine leaves in boiling water for 20 minutes to remove salt.

Fry onion until golden, add rice and fry for an additional 5 minutes, stirring constantly. Add pine nuts and stir for 3 more minutes.

Remove from heat and add meat, tomato sauce and seasonings.

Put 2 tsp of the mixture in each leaf, fold over two sides and roll up from stem side to opposite edge.

Put stuffed leaves in a casserole, folded side facing down. Cover with water plus 2 tbsp lemon juice, $^1/_2$ tsp salt and 1 tbsp oil. Bring to a boil and simmer for 45-60 minutes over a low heat. Add more water if necessary.

Can be eaten hot or cold. Ideal for cocktails.

Taboulleh

When searching for a grain-based salad that's originally Arabian, tangy and refreshing, nothing beats Taboulleh. This salad is part of the diet of Arab countries located along the Fertile Crescent. Eating Taboulleh is a wonderful way to ease the heavy taste of grilled meats and fish. Made from burghul - cracked wheat - and chopped herbs, it's all that it's cracked up to be!

INGREDIENTS

(6 servings)

2 cups fine burghul (cracked wheat)

4 cubed tomatoes

1 cup finely chopped parsley

2 tbsp finely chopped mint

6 sliced spring onions

3 tbsp olive oil

4 tbsp lemon juice

1 tsp salt

$^1/_4$ tsp pepper

PREPARATION

■ *Cover burghul wheat with boiling water. Let stand for 30 minutes until water is absorbed. If necessary, drain and dry with paper towels.*

■ *Add tomatoes, onions, parsley and mint.*

■ *Add remaining ingredients and refrigerate. Toss well before serving.*

Soups

Cooking soup is not only an art, it is also a fine example of how several cultures are blended together in one vessel. Israelis of European descent are traditionally bound to serving soups as a first or second course in every main meal. Hot light soups such as chicken or vegetable, are the usual bill-of-fare. Even on sultry summer days, soups - albeit cold - remain part-and-parcel of daily dining. On the other hand, Israelis rooted to North Africa are not accustomed to including soups as an introductory course on their main menu. Rather, they view soup as a meal in itself, accompanied by bread for dunking purposes. Cold, wet, wintry days call for rich, meaty soups resembling stews. The cooking process is a slow, simmering one starting in the morning, continuing throughout the day. Each family member coming home chilled to the bone, takes solace in knowing that a hot bowl of thick soup is always waiting.

Lentil Soup

Lentil soup has played an integral role in the Jewish culinary tradition ever since Esau sold his birthright to Jacob for a bowl of "Marak Adashim." All Israelis make lentil soup, regardless if their ancestry goes back to Europe or the Middle East. The difference lies in the condiments used for spicing it up. A thick, tasty soup, it is a standard feature on Israeli home and restaurant menus. Needless to say, lentil soup is a natural for a first course. During cold winter months it can be easily transformed into a rich lunch by adding sliced frankfurters into the soup and serving it with black bread and a salad on the side.

INGREDIENTS

(6-8 servings)
1½ cups washed green/brown lentils,
soaked overnight in 5 cups water
1 large diced onion
2 crushed garlic cloves
2 tbsp margarine
6-7 cups water
2 tsp beef soup powder or
2 beef stock cubes
1 tsp salt
½ tsp pepper
3 cubed medium potatoes
3 sliced frankfurters (optional)

PREPARATION

In a large pot, fry onions and garlic in margarine for 5 minutes, stirring often until soft.
Drain lentils. Add to the pot and fry for another 2-3 minutes.
Add water, seasonings and beef stock. Bring to a boil, cover and simmer for an hour.
Add potatoes and cook for another 20 minutes, or until tender.
Add sausages or smoked meat and cook for another few minutes.

Oriental Bone Soup

Make no bones about it, this soup is one of the more delicious and exotic dishes Israelis serve up. It is ideal for a Sabbath or holiday meal. While this recipe hails from the Middle East, bear in mind that Ashkenazi Jews have their own variation which calls for different spices.

INGREDIENTS

(6 servings)
6-8 pieces of beef or calves feet
9 cups water
2 tbsp salt
1 tsp white pepper
2 bay leaves
1 tsp cumin
2 tbsp beef soup powder
4 chopped garlic cloves
2 sliced carrots
3 large sliced onions
2 sliced celery sticks
2 sliced tomatoes (optional)
3 large cubed potatoes

PREPARATION

Put bones and water into a large pan and bring to a boil. Skim.

Add remaining ingredients, except for potatoes. Simmer covered for 3½ hours.

Add potatoes and cook covered for another 20 minutes.

Remove bay leaves. Serve piping hot with pita or black bread.

NOTE: It is best to make this soup the day before serving so that you can refrigerate it and skim off the top layer of fat before reheating.

Balkan Yogurt Cucumber Soup

Israelis love eating yogurt. A rainbow of yogurt goods can be found in all supermarkets and local groceries. To name a few: there are yogurts with fruit, yogurts with granola, yogurts with honey. Then there are vanilla, strawberry, blueberry, even chocolate flavored yogurts. Finally there are those yogurts which have 0% fat content, 1.5%, 3% and even 5%. With so many products on the market, yogurt has become a natural ingredient for "spin-off" dishes - such as this cool summer soup.

INGREDIENTS

(4 servings)
4 small plain yogurt containers
¼ cup white wine vinegar
3-4 ice cubes (optional)
3 crushed garlic cloves
3 tbsp chopped dill
3 tbsp olive oil
1 tsp salt
4 small cucumbers, washed,
dried & diced
¼ cup chopped walnuts (optional)

PREPARATION

Pour yogurts into a bowl and add vinegar and ice cubes. Stir well.

Add garlic, dill, olive oil and salt. Adjust seasoning.

Add diced cucumber and mix all ingredients together.

Refrigerate for several hours. Serve cold garnished with dill and walnuts.

Hot Avocado Soup

Israelis are adept at creating numerous avocado recipes. They've discovered that the fruit is so versatile, it can even be liquefied. This blend of avocado, wine and chicken is an original Israeli creation developed by the country's younger chefs, and makes for an interesting and exotic soup.

INGREDIENTS

(3-4 servings)
4 cups chicken broth
(can be made from a powdered mix)
2 large avocados
1 cup white wine
3 tbsp lemon juice
salt & white pepper to taste
chives and croutons for garnish

PREPARATION

Prepare the chicken soup.
Halve the avocados and scoop out the flesh.
Blend hot chicken soup and avocados in food processor until smooth.
Add remaining ingredients and gently heat over a low flame. **Do not boil**, *as avocado becomes bitter.*
Serve immediately, garnished with croutons and chives.

Honeyed Tomato Soup

*Israel was originally charac-
terized in the Bible as "a land
flowing with milk and honey."
At the time, the country's main
honey was a thick syrup made
from either grapes or dates.
The tradition of viewing honey
as a delicacy has been carried
on throughout the centuries. On
Rosh Hashana, Jews traditionally dip their bread in honey to
symbolize the wish for a sweet
new year. Today, Israel is
renowned for its honey and
sweet traditions.*

INGREDIENTS

(4-6 servings)
1 cup chopped onions
2 tsp salt
4 chopped garlic cloves
4 tbsp oil
1 cup water
$^{1}/_{2}$ tsp pepper
2 tbsp honey
5 cups (1 liter) tomato juice
Garnish: croutons or cream

PREPARATION

Fry onions and garlic with salt in the oil for 5 minutes until they look translucent.

Add remaining ingredients and simmer covered for 20 minutes.

If a smooth consistency is preferred, blend.

Serve hot either with croutons, or a tsp sour or whipping cream in center of each portion.

Fish

Israel's diverse ethnic blend provides the bait for numerous fish recipes. A staple of every holiday, Israelis look to their ethnic roots in preparing fish as an appetizer. Those of European descent carp over the thought of not having a portion of gefilte fish for their Sabbath or holiday meals. Their Levantine counterparts have a more spicy outlook. They'll take a nice piece of trout or perch, season it with a variety of zesty herbs and condiments, and either bake or fry it.

Israel's balmy, sunny climate permits for many months of outside fish dining by the sea. Families relax by the water and grill fresh fish garnished with native herbs and spices. The crispy skin and moist meat of charcoaled fish is a tantalising palate pleaser.

Other Israelis adopt the Arab tradition of preparing it taboun style – smeared with oil and lemon juice, seasoned with herbs and spices, and baked in a moderately heated oven.

In fact, the fresh fish bill-of-fare has spawned numerous fish restaurants patronized by tourists in cities such as Jaffa, Tiberias, Acre, Caesarea and Eilat.

Tiberias Fish a la Tehina

Here's a typical fish dish spawned in Tiberias. It's made with Israel's famous St. Peter's fish - a strain originally found in the Sea of Galilee and presently bred in northern fish farms. Note the definite Middle Eastern twist to this recipe. A dash of ingenuity prompted Israeli chefs to take a favorite dip and drip (not dip) it over the fish. It is served along with taboulleh, eggplant slices and olives.

INGREDIENTS

(4 servings)
Marinade: $^1/_2$ cup lemon juice
4 crushed garlic cloves
salt & pepper to taste

4 small-medium cleaned trout
or St. Peter's Fish
$^1/_2$ cup all-purpose flour
1 cup oil for frying
$1^1/_2$ cups tehina paste
5 tbsp lemon juice
3 crushed garlic cloves
3 tbsp chopped parsley
water as needed
$^1/_2$ cup fried blanched
almonds & parsley for garnish

PREPARATION

Mix lemon juice, garlic, salt & pepper and marinade the trout in it for 3 hours, turning occasionally.
Remove fish and dry.
Dip each fish in flour and coat on both sides. Fry in hot oil in a wide skillet on both sides until golden. Drain on paper toweling.
Place fish side-by-side in an oven-proof dish.
Mix tehina paste with lemon juice, salt, pepper, garlic cloves and parsley, adding water until a thick sauce is formed. Pour over fish.
Bake 15 minutes in a medium-hot oven, until golden-brown and bubbly.
Garnish with almonds and parsley, and serve immediately.

Libyan Fried Fish in Tomato Sauce

Tomatoes and tomato by-products constitute a growing export sector in Israel's food industry. To date, Israel exports close to $40 million worth of tomato goods. This includes fresh juices, pastes, peeled and diced tomatoes, plus sauces. Speaking of sauces, this recipe is a saucy idea on how to dress up a fish dish. While it calls for tomato sauce, the real sauciness lies in the use of beer in the batter.

INGREDIENTS

(4 servings)
1¹/₂ lb (750 g) of Hake,
Halibut or Perch fillets
oil for frying
Batter:
1 cup all-purpose flour
1 cup beer (or more if necessary)
1 egg
1 tbsp oil
salt & pepper to taste
Sauce:
3 tbsp olive oil
1 large chopped onion
2 chopped garlic cloves
14 oz. (420 g) can crushed tomatoes
1 cup water
1 tbsp capers
1 tsp dried or 1 tbsp fresh rosemary,
basil or thyme

PREPARATION

Wash and dry fish. Cut into serving size pieces.

Mix all batter ingredients in a bowl to a medium-thick batter.

Dip pieces of fish in batter and fry in oil on both sides until golden brown. Drain on paper towels.

In a separate pan, fry the onion and garlic in olive oil over a medium heat for about 7 mins. stirring until soft.

Add the tomatoes, salt, pepper, herbs and water and simmer for around 20 minutes.

Place the fried fish in a casserole, pour tomato sauce over it, garnish with capers and bake for 30 minutes in a medium oven.

Serve hot, or at room temperature, with rice or noodles.

Moroccan Spicy Pepper Fish

Jewish folklore provides some added spice to marine life. For instance, fish are a sign of good luck because they are the zodiac sign of the Jewish month of Adar, when Purim is celebrated. Consequently, Middle Eastern Jews used fish designs for amulets to ward off wicked spirits. Their Eastern European counterparts often named baby boys "Fishl" as a good omen against the evil eye. For a more tangible way of spicing up fish folklore there are fabled recipes like this one, which calls for cooking the fish on top of the oven instead of baking it.

INGREDIENTS

(4-5 servings)
2 lbs fish (900 g) either Perch,
Halibut or Hake
1 large sliced onion
2 sliced tomatoes
2 sliced red peppers
1 sliced green pepper
1 sliced yellow pepper (if available)
1-2 chopped hot peppers (optional)
1 tsp salt
1 tsp black pepper
1 tbsp red paprika - hot or sweet
1 tbsp fish spice
$\frac{1}{2}$ cup oil
3-4 chopped garlic cloves
$\frac{1}{2}$ cup chopped parsley
water to cover

PREPARATION

Wash and dry fish, and cut into 4 portions.
Mix tomatoes and peppers. Place half on the
bottom of a wide pan. Place fish on top and
cover with remaining vegetables.
Mix spices with oil and pour on top. Sprinkle
with parsley and garlic. Barely cover with water.
Cover pan and simmer over a low flame for
one hour. To thicken sauce, remove fish and
vegetables and boil uncovered for a few more
minutes.
Pour over fish.
Serve hot or at room temperature, garnished
with chopped parsley.

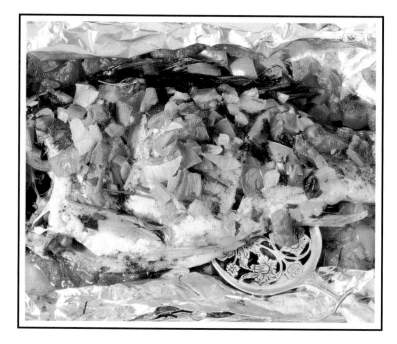

Barbecued or Baked Carp

Some countries have a national bird. We have a national fish which everyone loves to cook. In fact, there's a lot of carping if it's missing on a Sabbath or holiday menu. Naturally, it's all a matter of style. Ashkenazim use ground carp for making "gefilte fish". They also like to boil it along with onions, carrots and herbs, chill it and serve it cold. Sephardim, on the other hand, are more prone to baking carp and serving it hot.

INGREDIENTS

(4 servings)
2 large or 4 medium carp
4 chopped ripe tomatoes
2 sliced onions
2 sliced green peppers
5 crushed garlic cloves
2 tbsp parsley
1 tbsp dill
1 tbsp kusbara (optional)
3 tbsp olive oil
3 tbsp dry white wine
salt & pepper to taste

PREPARATION

Wash, clean and dry the fish, and make three slashes on each side. Brush each fish with olive oil both inside and outside.

Mix all vegetables and seasonings.

Prepare a sheet of aluminum foil large enough to pack the fish in, either individually or all together.

Put half the quantity of vegetables on the foil. Place fish on top. Fill the stomach and slashes of the fish with vegetables and put the rest on top of the fish.

Sprinkle fish with wine. Loosely fold all sides of the foil, leaving room for the fish to swell, and place in pan.

Barbecue, or bake in a medium oven for 45-50 minutes. If barbecuing, double the layer of foil.

Meats

In Israel the preparation of both meat and poultry is as close as one can get to an ethnic cuisine. Regardless of their origins, all Israelis are expert at making a variety of stuffed, roasted, broiled and baked chicken recipes.

Thanks to Israel's melting pot, Israelis are no longer in a stew over what to make for the Sabbath. Stewing is what they do best - from the famous European cholent, to the renowned Moroccan couscous and Iraqi kubeh. Slow - cooked foods, they are meant to be eaten at a leisurely pace so that diners savor every mouthful.

Lamb dishes evoke echoes of Bedouin hospitality. While some recipes are baked, many call for an open grill or spit. In fact, outdoor barbecuing is a favorite pastime among all Israelis - especially when on vacation or celebrating the holidays. Israelis love being outside. Families pack into their cars, drive to specific destinations, follow nature paths, and set up shop in designated forest picnic areas. Equipped with portable barbecues, bags of charcoal, disposable spits, and compact all-in-one picnic tables with attached benches, they unload a host of yummy marinated meats and get grilling.

INGREDIENTS

(4 servings)
4 pieces turkey or chicken breast
(about 125g or 4ozs each)
1 tbsp. lemon juice
$^1/_2$ tsp. salt
$^1/_4$ tsp. pepper
1 egg
$^1/_2$ cup all-purpose flour
$^1/_2$ cup spiced breadcrumbs
$^1/_2$ cup sesame seeds
oil for frying

PREPARATION

Sprinkle turkey with lemon juice, salt and pepper. Let stand for 30 minutes.

Beat egg in a shallow dish.

Put flour on a wide plate.

Mix together bread crumbs with sesame seeds on a separate plate.

Dip turkey breasts in flour, then in the egg, and coat evenly with breadcrumb mixture.

Heat oil in a heavy frying pan and fry turkey pieces over a medium heat on both sides until golden brown. Drain on paper towels.

Serve hot with lemon wedges, potatoes or rice, and cooked vegetables.

Mediterranean Chicken in Olives

First mentioned in the book of Deuteronomy as one of Israel's seven species, olives have always played an important role in the country's culinary culture. To this day there are trees in Israel dating back 1,000 years which still produce the fruit. While olive trees blossom at the beginning of the summer, the fruit does not ripen until early October. Olive oil is used extensively in many Israeli recipes, while the olives themselves can be eaten cold or cooked, as shown in this Yemenite recipe.

INGREDIENTS

(4 servings)
1 large chicken cut into pieces
or 4 chicken joints
3 tbsp olive oil
1 large diced onion
2 crushed garlic cloves
3 large tomatoes, peeled and
crushed (fresh or canned)
1 cup pitted green olives
3 tbsp tomato juice
1¼ cups chicken stock
or broth (powder or cube)
½ cup dry white wine

PREPARATION

■ *Pre-heat oven to 180⁰ c or 350⁰ f.*
Season chicken joints with salt and pepper and
bake in a greased baking pan for 20 minutes.
■ *Meanwhile, in a heavy pot, fry onion and garlic*
in oil for about seven minutes until soft.
■ *Add remaining ingredients. Cook covered on a*
low heat for about 10 minutes.
■ *Remove chicken from oven and cover with fried*
onion and olive mixture.
■ *Bake covered with aluminium foil in a 170⁰c or*
325⁰f oven for 30 minutes.
■ *Uncover and bake for another 10 minutes.*
■ *Serve hot with rice, or pasta.*

Jaffa Orange Chicken

Considering the amount of chicken eaten in Israel, one would believe that Israelis are crying "fowl" a lot. Certainly, there's no fowl play where chicken is concerned. This recipe combines chicken with another national favorite- Jaffa oranges, still Israel's most popular "ambassador" abroad. Sweet potatoes or rice make for a perfect side dish.

INGREDIENTS

(4 servings)
1 chicken cut into pieces
4 tbsp marmalade,
preferably slightly warmed
3 tsp chicken soup powder
1 cup pineapple pieces
1 cup orange juice
2 peeled and sliced oranges
$\frac{1}{2}$ sliced lemon (optional)
1 tbsp cornflour
orange rind to garnish (optional)

PREPARATION

Place chicken pieces side-by-side, in a baking dish. Spread the marmalade all over the chicken and sprinkle with chicken soup powder.

Put the pineapple pieces around the chicken (above and below). Pour orange juice over the chicken.

Cover with aluminum foil and bake in a 170⁰-180⁰c or 350⁰f oven for 30 minutes, basting frequently.

Remove the aluminum foil, adjust seasoning and cover the chicken with the orange slices. If you like it slightly sour, add lemon slices. Bake for a further 30 minutes until soft and brown.

If a thicker sauce is required, put liquid from chicken in a pan and add 1 tbsp cornflour mixed with 2 tbsp orange juice. Boil until thickened and pour over chicken.

Garnish with orange slices and pineapple.

Couscous

Although couscous is actually a grain, its name has become synonymous with a complete meal. North Africa's national dish, couscous was first brought over to Israel in the 1950's by Morroccan and Tunisian immigrants. In essence, couscous bears the same importance to Sephardim as cholent does to Ashkenazim. Out of one pot comes forth a meal consisting of a soup, steamed grain, stewed meat or poultry or fish and cooked vegetables. World travelers have found that many couscous variations exist throughout North Africa. Each country and city has its own specific touch.

INGREDIENTS

(4-5 servings)
1 package couscous
$1^{1}/_{2}$ cups chickpeas, cooked or canned
1 chicken cut into 8 serving pieces
or 1 lb (450g) lamb, or half of each
3 tbsp oil, preferably olive oil
2 chopped onions
4-6 carrots
4-6 celery stalks
4-6 courgettes
1 lb (450 g) pumpkin, peeled and
cut in medium squares
$^{1}/_{2}$ small cabbage (optional)
2-3 tbsp chicken soup powder
salt & $^{1}/_{2}$ tsp black pepper
$^{1}/_{2}$ tsp hot paprika
garlic powder to taste

PREPARATION

■ *Heat oil in a large pan. Add chicken or meat and brown on all sides. Season with salt, pepper, paprika and garlic powder.*

■ *Add vegetables. Cover with water and bring to a boil. Add soup powder and adjust seasonings. Cover and simmer for about 40 minutes until vegetables and meat are tender.*

■ *Prepare couscous according to package instructions.*

■ *To serve: Pile the couscous onto a large plate and place meat or chicken and vegetables on top. Put the soup in a separate bowl and the chickpeas in another small bowl. For each serving, put some couscous with meat and vegetables on a plate, pour over some soup and sprinkle with chickpeas.*

S i n i y e

A traditional Arab and Druse dish made from ground lamb, herbs and spices, mixed together and pressed into a round baking dish, Siniyeh is served with salad and pickles. What makes Siniyeh so delicious is its unusual combination of spices, tehina sauce and chopped nuts. It is ideal as a piquant first course. Siniyeh is a culinary attraction of restaurants located in the Galilee.

INGREDIENTS

(4 servings as a main course)
2 lb (900g) minced lamb
$1/2$ cup finely chopped onion
$1/2$ cup finely chopped parsley
2 crushed garlic cloves
2 tbsp flour or bread crumbs
$1/4$ cup olive oil
$1/8$ tsp nutmeg
$1/4$ tsp cumin
$1/2$-1 tsp salt
$1/2$ tsp pepper
$1/8$ tsp cinnamon
Topping: $3/4$ cups tehina paste
5 tbsp lemon juice
$1/2$ cup or more of water
2 crushed garlic cloves
$1/2$ tsp salt
$1/4$ tsp black pepper
2 tbsp pine nuts
few drops of olive oil

PREPARATION

▪ *Pre-heat oven to 190^0 c or 375^0 f.*
▪ *Mix all the ingredients (apart from the topping), adjust seasoning and put in a round, well-greased 22 cm ($8^1/2$") heat-proof dish, or 4 individual greased oven-proof dishes. Bake for 15 minutes.*
▪ *Mix tehina with lemon juice, water, salt, pepper, garlic and parsley, and spread over meat. Return to oven and bake for 10 minutes more.*
▪ *Sprinkle pine nuts on top and bake for another 5 minutes.*
▪ *Serve hot, garnished with chopped parsley and a few drops of olive oil.*

Hungarian Meat Goulash

In the Talmudic period, meat was regarded as the diet of the rich. It never appeared on the daily menu. Instead, it was saved for festive occasions and holidays. Since meat was also associated with joy, it was also served every Sabbath. With Israelis rooted to so many countries around the globe, numerous Sabbath meat recipes abound. Goulash, a popular Hungarian meat course, is loved by all. Israel boasts many goulash variations, including Moroccan goulash. This recipe, however, is akin to the original Hungarian formula.

INGREDIENTS

(6-8 servings)
3 lbs (1,350 g) cubed beef
2 tbsp all-purpose flour
3 tbsp oil
2 large chopped onions
5 crushed garlic cloves
$1/2$ cubed green pepper
$1/2$ cubed red pepper
1 small carrot peeled and sliced
3 diced tomatoes
$1^1/2$ cups tomato sauce or juice
1 bay leaf
salt & pepper to taste
$1^1/2$ tsp paprika
1 cup beef broth
(made from a can or a cube)

PREPARATION

Roll the beef in flour and fry in oil on all sides until brown. Remove from pan.

In the same oil gently fry the onions and garlic, for about 10 minutes stirring often, until they are very soft. Add peppers, carrot and tomatoes.

Return meat to pan. Add tomato sauce, seasonings and stock. Cover and cook gently over a very low flame until soft, for at least 1 - $1^1/2$ hours. Season to taste and remove bay leaf.

Serve on a bed of rice. As an added option, mix rice with peas.

Variation: For a complete "meal in a dish" add 3 large peeled and cubed potatoes to the meat when it is almost soft. Cook for a further 15 minutes, or until the potatoes are done.

Side Dishes

No main course in Israel is complete without a hot vegetable, grain or starch. Israelis often smother vegetables in a tasty sauce which at times is topped with a variety of nuts or crisp onions for added crunchiness. Numerous vegetable variations abound. While vegetable-based kugels are still considered side dishes, quiches made from fresh produce are often served as a main course.

Israelis adhering to their North African cooking traditions frequently stuff an assortment of vegetables, such as onions and squash. While Europeans fill peppers with mixtures made from meat, rice and onions, they also "stuff" cabbage by placing a favorite meat concoction in the center of a leaf, and then rolling it. These vegetable dishes are so satiating that they are often used as substitutes for the main course.

Grains, on the other hand, are usually served dry. Israelis stemming from both the East and West have devised a host of rice recipes. On its own, couscous is a favorite grain for accompanying any main course. And potatoes? Here every Israeli sees eye to eye.

Cauliflower Kugel

A filling vegetable dish with its own distinctive flavor, this kugel harks back to the European tradition of transforming vegetables into tasty casseroles. If you or your family don't like cauliflower, you can use broccoli instead.

INGREDIENTS

(8 servings)
1 large fresh cauliflower
or 2 lbs frozen cauliflower
3 eggs
3 tbsp mayonnaise
3 tbsp onion
or mushroom soup powder
pinch of nutmeg
1 tbsp flour

PREPARATION

■ *Cook cauliflower until tender. Drain and mash with a fork.*

■ *Add eggs, mayonnaise, soup powder, and flour. Thoroughly mix together.*

■ *Pour into a greased 9"x12" (22x30 cms) baking pan.*

■ *Cover and bake in a moderate oven for 20 minutes. Uncover and continue baking for another 10 minutes, or until golden.*

■ *Cut into squares and serve hot.*

Courgettes (Squash) in Tomato Sauce

Squash any erroneous notions about vegetables being boring. There is certainly nothing dull about a combination of sauteed onions, brown sugar, sweet pepper and olives. Once this dish is made it can either be served as a hot side dish, chilled and served cold as part of a salad meal, or with a cool main course.

INGREDIENTS

(6 servings)
6 medium courgettes
or 12 small ones
3 tbsp olive oil
³/₄ cup chopped onions
2 chopped garlic cloves
2 peeled and chopped tomatoes
1 cubed red pepper
¹/₂ cubed green pepper
¹/₂ tsp brown sugar
¹/₂ cup chopped olives
3 tbsp tomato sauce
¹/₂ cup water
salt and pepper to taste
pinch of thyme (dried or fresh)

PREPARATION

Wash and dry courgettes and remove stems.

In a large, deep pot heat the oil and fry onions and garlic for about 7 minutes, stirring occasionally.

Add peppers and chopped tomatoes and fry for another 3 minutes.

Sprinkle with sugar and stir.

Add courgettes. Cover and cook over low-medium heat for 15 minutes turning occasionally.

Stir in olives, tomato sauce and water and cook until soft.

Uncover and cook until some of the liquid has evaporated.

For a dairy meal serve with sour cream, yogurt or grated parmesan cheese.

Potato Latkes

In Eastern Europe, Jewish cuisine was based on two staples - black bread and potatoes. Housewives used potatoes as the main ingredient for a variety of dishes. Potatoes were often eaten in various forms two or three times a day. They were served baked, cooked with onions and pepper, fried, or mashed with chicken fat. Little wonder that another variation - potato latkes - has become a popular staple for festive meals and holidays such as Hanukkah.

INGREDIENTS

(4 servings)
4 large, medium-grated potatoes
1 small grated onion
2 beaten eggs
3 tbsp all-purpose flour
1 tsp baking powder
1 tsp salt to taste
½ tsp freshly ground black pepper
oil for deep frying

PREPARATION

■ *Drain grated potatoes in a colander for fifteen minutes. Transfer to a bowl.*

■ *Add eggs, flour, baking powder and seasonings. Mix well.*

■ *Heat oil in a large frying pan. Drop tablespoons of the mixture into the hot oil and fry on both sides until golden brown.*

Drain on paper towels.

■ *Serve hot with apple sauce or sour cream and sugar.*

Guvetch

Wherever Jews have lived, they have adopted the country's culinary practices, adapting them to kosher dietary laws. Today, many of these dishes are considered part-and-parcel of Jewish cuisine. For instance, in Poland the delicacies that were eaten were lokshen, stuffed or stewed fish. Today the lokshen is known as noodles and the stuffed fish - gefilte fish! Another Polish dish made popular in Israel is guvetch. Certainly no one kvetches about it. A concoction composed of a variety of vegetables, this dish summons up only compliments.

INGREDIENTS

(4-6 servings)
1 large onion
1 medium eggplant
1 large courgette (squash or zucchini)
4 tomatoes
1 green pepper
1 red pepper
1 yellow pepper (optional)
1 small diced hot pepper (optional)
4 tbsp olive oil
5 tbsp tomato sauce or juice
$^1/_4$ cup water
$^1/_2$ tsp sugar
salt and black pepper to taste
soup powder to taste

PREPARATION

Cut all the vegetables into 1-1$^1/_2$" (2$^1/_2$-3$^1/_2$ cms) cubes.

Heat oil in a large pan and add all the vegetables. Stir over a moderate heat for a few minutes.

When all the oil has been absorbed, lower the heat and add the tomato sauce, water and seasonings. Cover and simmer gently for $^1/_2$ an hour, stirring occasionally. If preparation appears to be drying out, add a little more water.

Adjust seasonings.

Can be eaten hot or cold. The dish should be juicy and the vegetables very soft.

Almond Raisin Rice

North Africans love to embellish their rice dishes with assorted ingredients. A combination of raisins and nuts adds a sweet flavor and crunchy texture to the rice. This particular recipe is popular among all Israelis. It is typically served at weddings and festive feasts. It is also a variation of a stuffing often used for filling chickens.

INGREDIENTS

(4 servings)
1 cup white rice, washed and drained
2 tbsp margarine or olive oil
1 chopped onion
2 cups boiling water
1 tbsp chicken soup powder
$^1/_2$ cup raisins
$^1/_2$ cup slivered almonds
1 tbsp oil

PREPARATION

Fry the onion in margarine, stirring occasionally for about 7-10 minutes, until soft and golden.

Add rice and fry for 5 minutes, stirring constantly, until the rice begins to brown.

Add boiling water and soup powder, cover and cook on a very low heat for close to 10 minutes.

Add raisins and cook for another 7-10 minutes until rice is soft and most of the water has been absorbed. Cover and let stand for 10 minutes.

Fry almonds in oil until light brown and add to the rice. Mix and serve hot.

Variation: Instead of raisins, add $^1/_2$ cup chopped dill and leave out almonds. Turn off heat and leave to stand for $^1/_2$ hour.

Mejadra

Rooted in the Middle East, Mejadra is considered a specialty of Israel's Galilean Arab community. In countries around the Middle East, both rice and lentils are placed in large open sacks and sold in outdoor markets. Since these two food staples are stored in homes for long time periods, household chefs have composed a variety of dishes around them. Mejadra is one of them. A delicious grain combination, it is served either as a side dish for meat main courses, or combined with fresh yogurt for dairy meals.

INGREDIENTS

(6-8 servings)
1 cup brown lentils soaked overnight
1 cup brown rice
2 cups water
1 tsp soup powder
½ tsp salt
½ tsp pepper
½ tsp cumin
2 large finely chopped onions
3 tbsp olive oil
½ tsp lemon juice (optional)

PREPARATION

Cover lentils with salted water and cook for about 45 minutes, until soft. Drain.

Put rice, water, soup powder, salt and pepper and cumin in a pan. Bring to a boil and cook for about 15-20 minutes, until all moisture is absorbed and rice is tender.

Fry onions in olive oil until golden.

Combine lentils, rice and onions. Adjust seasonings. Reserve some fried onion for garnish and serve hot.

Desserts

Here's an interesting tidbit about the final course of a typical Israeli repast, whether it be at home or in a restaurant. It's usually light, refreshing, and often fruity. Israel's Garden of Eden has yielded such a wide array of citrus, deciduous and exotic fruits that Israelis are wont to sink their teeth into succulent, vitamin-filled food at the end of their meal. Fresh fruit salads, compote, baked apples, or a juicy slice of watermelon are very often the favorite finale.

Still, Israeli cooks are mindful of those who must satisfy the yearnings of a nagging sweet tooth. Fruits frequently provide the base for refreshing sherbets and whips, or liquor spiked dishes. Chocolate junkies indulge in the chocolate mousses served at home and in all restaurants.

There are typical Middle Eastern pastries: Baklava and Knaffe - small, sweet, and flaky, filled with honey and nuts; Ma'amoul - petite "cakes" made from a fatty dough and filled with dates and nuts; and Ba'ahbah - made from a dry dough loaded with dates and sesame seeds. Nonetheless, many Israelis prefer American/Continental style cakes because they are delicate, fluffy and elegant looking.

Sabra Oranges

Sabra, the nickname for a native Israeli, is derived from the sabra fruit. Thorny on the outside and soft on the inside, the fruit's characteristics are an apt description of the Israeli personality - especially during the country's formative years. Today, Israeli temperaments are a bit less prickly, as illustrated in this dessert delicacy.

INGREDIENTS

(4-6 servings)
4 oranges (preferably Jaffa if available)
$^3/_4$ cup sugar
$^1/_4$ cup water
$^1/_2$ cup orange juice
$^1/_4$ cup lemon juice
2 tbsp "Sabra" liquor, or brandy,
or other orange liqueur

PREPARATION

Thinly pare rind off two oranges and slice into narrow strips.

Peel remaining oranges. Thinly slice all four into a glass bowl. Sprinkle oranges with "Sabra" or brandy.

Bring remaining ingredients to a boil and add rind. Simmer until the peel is almost transparent (about 20 mins.).

Pour the hot syrup and peel over the orange slices and cool.

Serve at room temperature, decorated with strawberries or cherries, with or without whipping cream.

Strawberry Sherbet

Strawberries are in season in Israel between the months of December and May. Their quality is among the best in the world and their popularity is so great that they are sold on street corners and roadside stands in kilo bags and cartons of all sizes. Once strawberries hit the market, farmers have a hard time keeping pace with the great demand. While Israelis make a variety of strawberry desserts, the typical way of eating the fruit is dipping it into a bowl of sugar and popping it in your mouth.

INGREDIENTS

(6-8 servings)
2 cups strawberries
washed and hulled
1 egg white
³/₄ cup sugar
1 tbsp lemon juice
6-8 strawberries and
mint leaves for garnish

PREPARATION

Blend strawberries with ¹/₂ cup sugar, in a blender or food processor.

Whip egg white until stiff, gradually adding remaining sugar.

Add strawberry mixture to the egg white in a steady stream, and continue beating for about 10 minutes until the quantity has almost doubled and is very fluffy.

Add lemon juice

Serve immediately as a whip, or freeze and serve as sherbet. Garnish with halved fresh strawberries and mint leaves.

Cheese Blintzes

Traditionally, blintzes are associated with Shavuot. Rolled pancakes filled with cheese, fruit or both, they make a delicious dessert. Israelis have expanded the blintz tradition by creating two categories: sweet and salty. Salty blintzes are made with a variety of vegetable fillings - from spinach and mushroom, to eggplant and broccoli. Sweet blintzes carry on the tradition of cheese and fruit fillings. Since both variations have become so popular, specialty blintz restaurants serving up a total blintz meal from start to finish, are now found in every Israeli city.

INGREDIENTS

(about 20 pieces)
Batter:
1 cup all purpose flour
$^3/_4$ cup milk
$^1/_2$ cup water or soda water
3 eggs
3 tbsp oil or melted butter
$^1/_2$ tsp salt
Filling:
1 lb or 450 g cream cheese
2 egg yolks
3-4 tbsp sugar
1 tbsp grated lemon peel
$^1/_2$ tsp vanilla extract
$^1/_4$ tsp cinnamon
$^1/_2$ cup raisins
oil for frying

PREPARATION

Mix batter ingredients until smooth and creamy.

Lightly coat a 6" or 8" (15 or 20 cms) frying pan (preferably non-stick) with oil and heat.

Pour a small amount of batter (about 2 tbsp) into pan. Swirl around until even and heat. When sides begin to curl away, turn and lightly fry blintz on other side for a few seconds only. Put onto a plate.

Repeat until all batter is used up.

Mix filling ingredients together. Put 2-3 tsp in each blintz (depending upon size), turn in sides and roll up like an envelope.

Before serving: Fry prepared blintzes very carefully in butter or spread melted butter on top and heat in oven. Serve either with sour cream and powdered sugar, maple or chocolate syrup.

Date Crisps

With so many date palm trees all over Israel, it's little wonder that a variety of date products are sold in supermarkets. Children love this dried fruit and all its spin-off creations. Consequently, housewives buy dried dates, date spreads and mashed dates for cooking and baking. Here's a novel recipe combining dates with another classic - rice crispies.

INGREDIENTS

(20 pieces)
1 cup (stick) margarine
(200g or 7-8 ozs)
$^1/_2$ cup sugar
2 tbsp honey
1 lb pitted, chopped dates
8 cups rice crispies
$^1/_4$ cup + 2 tbsp coconut

PREPARATION

Cook together first four ingredients and stir gently until well blended (about 10 mins.)

Remove from heat, add rice crispies and $^1/_4$ cup coconut. Mix thoroughly.

Place in a 10"x12"(25x30cms) pan. Flatten.

Sprinkle with 2 tbsp coconut and cut into squares.

Can be kept covered in the refrigerator for weeks.

Khada'if

*One of the grandest Medi-
terranean and Balkan dessert
cakes, Khada'if is light, crisp
and delicate. No bakery in the
Middle East is without it, and
neither is any celebration.
While the original recipe calls
for flour and water used in a
complicated baking process to
create a noodly appearance,
we have eliminated the bother
by using very thin noodles at
the start.*

INGREDIENTS

(15 pieces)
5 cups thinnest possible noodles
4 oz (100 gm) + 1 tbsp butter
5 tbsp sugar
1 cup coarsely chopped
nuts or almonds
1 cup whipping cream
1 cup milk
1 package instant vanilla pudding

PREPARATION

Melt the butter in a large pan and add noodles, sugar and almonds. Fry until light brown, stirring constantly.

Whip the cream with the instant pudding and milk (you can use 2 cups whipping cream with $\frac{1}{2}$ cup sugar).

Line a 10"x14" (25x35cm) dish with half the noodle mixture. Pour the cream over the noodles and spread the remaining noodle mixture on top.

Cover with foil and refrigerate. Must be eaten within 2-3 days.

Baklava

A crisp, honeyed sweet Arab pastry, Baklava is a typical Middle Eastern dessert. When served in restaurants, it is accompanied by a glass of mint tea or Turkish coffee. A layered cake made with nuts and topped with a sweet syrup, Baklava gives an elaborate appearance. But as they say, "never judge a book by its cover." Baklava may look complicated, but it is quite easy to prepare.

INGREDIENTS

1¹/₂ lb (750 gm) filo dough
¹/₂ lb (500 gm) peanuts, walnuts,
almonds or a mixture, roasted in
the oven, peeled and medium
chopped in food processor
7 ozs (200 gm) melted butter
¹/₂ cup sugar
1 tsp cinnamon
Topping:
2 cups sugar
³/₄ cup water
1¹/₂ tbsp lemon juice
¹/₂ tsp cinnamon

PREPARATION

Divide the dough into three equal parts. Line a greased 27x 35 cm (10¹/₂ x 13¹/₂ ") pan with ¹/₃ of the dough. Brush each filo sheet with melted butter (cover remaining dough with a damp towel to prevent it from drying out)

Mix the nuts with the sugar & cinnamon and sprinkle half the quantity over the dough.

Cover with another layer of brushed filo sheets, sprinkle the remaining nut mixture on top, and cover with the final layers of dough.

Cut into diamond shapes, but not all the way through.

Pour remaining butter on top.

Bake in a pre-heated medium-hot oven for ³/₄ hour, or until golden. Cut pieces through and allow to cool.

Prepare syrup for topping: boil all ingredients together until thick and pour over slightly cooled cake. Can be kept in the baking pan for several days, covered with aluminum foil.

Fruit Salad

In the book of Genesis, G-d says: "See I give you every seed... tree that has seed-bearing fruit; they shall be yours for food." Certainly Israel's founding fathers and ensuing generations have taken these words seriously. In the beginning they nurtured the country's famous Jaffa oranges and grapefruits. Today, Israel's cornucopia of fresh fruits dazzles the eye. Aside from lemons and pomellos, citrus growers have developed numerous strains of "easy peelers." Apple, pear, peach, nectarine, plum and grape orchards abound throughout the country, as do a variety of melon fields. The country's farmers have even taken to nurturing numerous exotic strains - such as persimmons, kiwis, and fijoyas.

INGREDIENTS

(6 servings)
1 melon, scooped into balls
4 black plums, cut into strips
3 cubed peaches
12 halved green grapes
15 halved black grapes
2 pears, peeled and cubed
(or any combination of
summer fruits desired)
2 tbsp pomegranate seeds
4 quartered fresh figs
$1/_4$ - $1/_2$ cup sugar
(depending how sweet your tooth is)
$1/_2$ cup cherry or other fruit brandy
$1/_2$ cup water

PREPARATION

Mix chosen fruits together into a bowl.

Cook sugar and water over a low flame until
sugar has melted. Add brandy.

Pour hot liquid over fruit. When cool,
refrigerate for a few hours.

Serve stuffed in empty melon shells, either
alone or with ice-cream or whipped cream.

Holidays

Even though we don't provide you with complete holiday menus, we do want you to "taste" the atmosphere, and get a feel for the way Israelis celebrate the festivals.

Tradition bound, Israeli families look to their ancestral heritage when planning their holiday menus. For instance, they tend to make a lot of tzimmis over their Rosh Hashana feasts. Honey- laced foods are the rule of the day and honey cake a national staple.

Succoth is one of the loveliest times of the year. Not only is the weather just right, but the enchanting array of beautiful succoth built on back lawns and balconies is truly a feast for the eyes. Putting up a succah is a family project, and succah hopping a traditional activity among neighbors. The pomegranate is a must for this holiday, which calls for dipping a new fruit in honey.

Comes Simchat Torah and the country's children

skip through the streets waving flags and bags of candy. Amid the dancing and the singing you'll find children licking, biting and chewing sugar coated apples eaten off a stick. This special treat appears once a year, making Simchat Torah a favorite among those with a sweet tooth.

Similarly, Hanukkah has its own sweet, distinctive touch - a round, holeless, sugar coated, jelly-filled doughnut sold by the dozens by street vendors, local supermarket owners and in the large hypermarkets. Eight days of eating doughnuts - however you slice it, that's a lot of dough!

Those who enjoy eating dried fruits take advantage of Tu 'Be'Shvat. A special Tu'Be'Shvat "seder" calls for platters of dried apricots, figs, dates, prunes, apples and banana slices. Vegetarians especially love this holiday because it legitimizes the use of carob delights for a variety of dishes.

As for Purim, we all know it is universally characterized by hamentashen and the exchanging of "Mishloach Manot." Nonetheless, in Israel Purim has an added twist, for the holiday spirit is felt a solid week before it actually takes place. Miniature Queen

Esthers, Mordechais, clowns, and magicians parade throughout the streets in their best finery, bringing a smile to everyone who passes by.

Certainly, Passover is the ultimate ethnic holiday. Israelis are steadfast about avoiding flour-based bread products. After all, Passover is the holiday when Matza - unleavened bread - rules the day. Admittedly, not all are thrilled about eating pure matza for a solid week. A little initiative has yielded a handful of recipes using matza meal for creating Passover hamburger and hot dog rolls as well as pizza dough! Many Israeli restaurants are closed during this holiday. The strict dietary restrictions make it far easier to shut down and take a week's vacation!

As soon as the Passover dishes have been tucked away for another year, mothers ready themselves for the next barrage - Lag Ba'Omer. The truth is, children have long been preparing for the great Lag Ba'Omer bonfire by collecting branches and wood. On Lag Ba'Omer eve everyone tightly closes their

shutters and windows in order to prevent soot from entering the house. Outside, around the blazing camp fires, parents and children roast potatoes, onions, and hot dogs. All enjoy the hardy victuals of this traditional evening barbecue.

Happily, Shavuot presents the welcome relief of a light, dairy meal. Certainly, blintzes are part of the Shavuot tradition. The Israeli twist comes with the assortment of cheese cakes and quiches.

Finally, Yom Ha'- Atzmaut - Independence Day - has its own culinary convention. When this day arrives it's time to make a "mangal" - an outdoor barbecue. The country's public parks are inundated with families. Parents cook on open grills while their children play catch. Shishlik meats which marinated overnight in a gravy are placed on long spits and grilled over the open fire. Ears of corn and potatoes are also plunked on top of the grill, and rotated until soft. Homemade salads are packed in containers and fresh pita breads are handed around to all. Dessert? Fresh fruit of course!

There's Never A Last Course

Israel's daily food feast literally lasts until the wee hours. Outdoor cafes are a popular feature in every city - large and small. Side-by-side with these cafes are a multitude of street vendors working the crowds from morning until night, serving up a quick morning bite, a drink on the run, mid-day snack or a late evening aperitif.

In some city sections, it's hard to escape the enticing aroma of favorite fast foods dished up at these sidewalk food stalls. Naturally, falafel is the preferred choice among those wishing to catch a quick but filling light meal. Shuarma - strips of turkey meat sitting on a large upright spit with lambs' fat dripping over it - is another pita-filled favorite. Vendors place a wide array of salads and dips on their counters, enabling customers to mix and match the meat with as many combinations as possible inside their bursting pita portion.

Quick snacks can be either hot or cold. For instance, pots of boiling corn are often strategically *positioned on heavily trafficked thoroughfares, with peddlars serving the corn in its ears and sprinkling salt on top.*

Similarly, hot bourekas sold in outdoor stands are popped in paper bags for people eating on the run. Freshly baked cheese-filled pastry crescents called "Sambousak" are favored among those catching a quick cup of coffee or cold beverage. Even hot bagels topped with sesame seeds or hyssop are a warm welcome, for people must make haste.

Naturally, all this food calls for a good drink. Israel is a pioneer in selling freshly squeezed carrot juice. Of course, oranges are compressed into thirst quenching drinks... as are a variety of other fruits.

Remember the question we asked in the beginning? "So, what's cooking in Israeli cuisine?" Decidedly, the answer is "a lot." Which is why you should come, see, smell and taste everything yourself In the meantime, this book is an excellent substitute for experiencing the "real thing." As they say in Hebrew "Beh'tay'avone." Hearty Appetite! Bon Appetit!

LIST OF RECIPES